A Day in Sark

The Island Tour

The Maseline jetty greets visitors arriving on Sark, a walk through a white concrete arch is necessary to the base of the harbour hill where a tractor drawn-bus, “the toast rack”, waits for those not wishing to walk up the steep 800m path which rises 90m to the top of the island. One may pause for refreshment at the harbour cafe, on the right, or travel straight on to visit the old harbour, accessible through another white tunnel (of 1866) to the left of the original rough entrance dug in 1588 by Philippe, son of the first Seigneur of Sark. Le Creux is older than Maseline and used by local fishermen and visiting yachtsmen; it is said to be one of the world’s smallest harbours and is certainly one of the most attractive. It may of course be visited last by those eager to see the rest of the Island.

Le Creux

Harbour Hill

Harbour Hill

The walk up Harbour Hill is steep but rewarded by interesting views, there is a path to the left, some 50m from the base, which directs one away from the noise and dust of the road. A similar path to the right is longer and steeper, leading to the north east of the Island, which people staying longer may find interesting. The main route parallels the road, rising through woodland with open views; in spring the path is bordered by abundant wild flowers. The top of the hill affords opportunities for respite: on the right the Aval du Creux Hotel and Restaurant, next to the Sark Electricity Company and set back from the road the Tourist Information Office. Immediately to the left of the path is the Bel Air Inn, with Sark's only off-licence, a landmark some never progress beyond. Above the Inn is the Founiais Restaurant and behind that is one of the Island's cycle hire stores.

The Base of Harbour Hill

A path in the centre of the Island

Walk, Cycle or Carriage?

Progress up the hill to La Collinette or crossroads. Here one should decide which way to see the Island. The central area may be accomplished in a pleasant stroll with lunch or tea added, and the possibility of some small exploration of shops, avenues and paths: a bicycle will open up the routes to North, West and South, while a carriage will achieve the same with slightly less expenditure of energy.

The horse-drawn carriages are on the left just before the Collinette and offer an hour or two with a knowledgeable guide in relaxed style; thesc may be pre-booked or approached on the day. There are bicycles for hire in any of three shops, behind the Founiais as already noted, straight ahead in the Avenue, or on the right a short way up Rue Lucas. Or you may simply wish to walk.

Carriages and La Collinette

The Avenue

Little Sark and La Coupée from The Hogs Back

From La Collinette

Directly ahead of La Collinette is The Avenue, Sark's principal shopping area which may be visited now or returned to after exploring.

There are two provisions shops, clothes and souvenir stores, Sark glass, the wood turner, cycle hire, perfumery, fishing tackle hire, the pottery, hairdressers, restaurants and the post office. To the left from La Collinette a road leads past one of the Islands two banks and after some 100m a turning to the right leads to Dixcart Bay and is one of the routes to Stocks and Dixcart Hotels. The main route is to Derrible Bay and the Hog's Back or the path over Les Lâches and back to the base of the Harbour Hill.

To explore the Island now continue from La Collinette right up Rue Lucas, north, where there are small restaurants, a pottery and silversmith and the museum.

Dixcart Bay

Lighthouse and offshore rocks (Grande Moie)

After 100m or so a turning seen to the right is Rue Hotton with a new stone house, La Marguerite on the corner, and, further on Aladdins Cave, the Mermaid Tavern, and a cycle hire shop.

Rue Hotton

For those with time and energy following the road to the end of Rue Hotton and turning left, leads either directly to a fine morning bay, La Grêve de la Ville, or after a few metres a right turn to the lighthouse (which is unfortunately not open to the public). One can also follow a path north to meet a road returning to Rue Lucas at Le Carrefour.

Le Carrefour

Garden and cottage at the North End

The North End

At Le Carrefour continue north up a tree-lined avenue passing the stamp collector's office on a sharp bend, to the area of Le Fort and Le Grand Fort, where there are some of Sark's oldest cottages, a beautiful garden, a working farm and carriage business and Sark's boat builders.

A path past the boat-yard leads to a headland with interesting cliff and sea views showing clockwise, Herm, Alderney, France, rocks to the east of Sark and the lighthouse. One of the cannons, part of the original Napoleonic fortifications, sits in a prominent place.

Go east from Le Grand Fort to a junction (with heart shaped roundabout) to the right (north again) is Eperquerie Common, an extensive area of grassy moorland with heather, bracken, many spectacular paths to the sea

At the Boat Builders

The West Coast of the Eperquerie

or landings and caves, and the remains of some Norman fortifications as well as more cannons. In spring the area has abundant and varied wild flowers; throughout the year there are wonderful sea views especially of Herm with the white strip of shell beach stretching north; further out a smudge on the horizon is Alderney.

Spring Flowers

The name Eperquerie alludes to the former use of the common for salting and drying of fish. Returning south from the Eperquerie roundabout after some 400m a path to the right can be followed to the "window in the rock," a 19th-century viewpoint cut in the cliff.

If time permits, further down the winding wooded path is a delightful secluded bay, Port du Moulin, with interesting and varied geological features, and views of the islands to the West.

South again, the gates to La Seigneurie will be seen on the right.

Window in the Rock

La Seigneurie

This is the residence of Sark's feudal head; the buildings date from 1675 with 18th and 19th century additions. It was first occupied as the Seigneurie in 1730 after Susan Le Pelley acquired the Fief and became the first Dame of Sark. The gardens have been extensively renovated and extended by the present Seigneur and Mrs Beaumont, and regularly win prizes and international acclaim for the colour and variety of their content and are a joy to walk round.

The Seigneurie grounds also house the Island's only dovecote, a battery with wartime relics, a pond and a maze.

Arch at the entrance to the Seigneurie field

Further Exploration, The Centre, West and Little Sark

Out of the Seigneurie gates to the south are a guest house and restaurant. The turning to the right for the Moinerie Hotel is marked by a signpost on one side and an arched stone gate on the other, the latter commemorating the Seigneur's silver wedding anniversary. It is the entrance to the field where the annual horse-show is held. The road ahead is crossed at Clos à Jaôn by the Rue du Sermon; left is a route back to La Collinette and Harbour, right, leads past Mon Plaisir store, the Methodist Chapel and Petit Champ Hotel then on to the Coupée and Little Sark. Immediately ahead at Clos à Jaôn is the senior school house, also used for meetings of the Island Parliament, followed by the Greffe Office, ambulance and fire stations, then the Island Hall with games, gifts and refreshment.

A little further is the 19th-century St Peter's Church with its tower. Past the church the road forks, left leads back to the Avenue and La Collinette, to the right further explores the Island down a tree lined lane joining the road from the Avenue immediately opposite the junior school, with tea

St Peter's Church

The 17th-Century Manoir

gardens on the left. At the end of the school furthest from the road is the tiny barrel-vaulted prison with two cells, available for use to a maximum of two days. The long low building on the right is the original 16th-century Manoir, it was built by and housed the first Seigneur, Helier de Carteret, it also incorporated the school and a chapel. Around the sharp right hand bend is the 17th-century Manoir in classic Jersey farmhouse style this was the residence of the Seigneur until the 1730's. Just past the Manoir a path leads to the left down a wooded and sometimes sheep-grazed valley with another route to Stocks and Dixcart Hotels.

Prison

Ahead is the blacksmith, an art gallery, a tea garden and the Mill, the latter built in 1571 by the first Seigneur, whose heraldic arms may just be seen on the lintel, it has weathered the years, though no sails remain. The mill is the highest point on the Island, the Germans made use of it as an observation post during the Second World War and it has been an arts and crafts gallery, now it is usually rented accommodation.

The Route to the Mill

Pilcher Monument

The road to Petit Champ

The staggered junction at the end of the road leads right to Petit Champ Hotel and back to Rue du Sermon or across the junction past the duck pond either left to Beauregard and a walk down Happy Valley or straight on to the Pilcher Monument. Here is the only place where all the main Channel Islands may be seen together.

Returning from the monument a path leads left to the Gouliot Headland and Caves, the latter a spectacular experience for those interested in marine zoology.

Back to the staggered junction a right turn leads towards Little Sark, passing award winning tea gardens, a turning on the left, again, to Dixcart and Stocks Hotels or a path to the right back to Pilcher Monument.

In the Gouliot Caves

La Coupée looking towards Little Sark

Grande Grêve, the Gouliot Headland and Brecqhou from La Coupée

After passing about a kilometre of cultivated fields, stone houses, sea views (and the kitchen of the chocolate maker) is La Coupée, the narrow isthmus some 60m high joining Little Sark to Sark. The west side falls to Sark's largest sandy beach, La Grande Grêve and has a spectacular view of the coast and other islands.

The east side is not negotiable but shows offshore rocks including L'Etac and in the distance Jersey and France. Visitors with energy will follow La Coupée to Little Sark. Of all the unspolit parts of Sark this is possibly the least changed by time, it has an air of rural tranquillity and the wildlife and wild flowers are plentiful.

The route towards Little Sark

Spring

Summer

Little Sark

There is one hotel, La Sablonnerie, originally a beamed 16th-century farmhouse, and an associated tea garden.

Paths with wild flowers lead to bays and bathing pools, a rugged coastline and a varied habitat for wildlife, views of the derelict silver mines and the landings at Port Gorey and Rouge Terrier.

View of the Silver Mine ruins towards Port Gorey

Looking West from La Coupée

The Bon Marin and the East Coast

You can see a lot of Sark in a day; a week or two will give the chance for exploration of more paths, coasts and bays. Some might say a year is not enough to see it all.

For those able to stay longer see:

Sark, a Photographic Guide by Chris Andrews and David Huelin published by Gateway Publishing Limited Sark.